# POLIGION
## The burning truth about non-taxation of the church

# KELLY LYNN

ISBN: 1456414186
ISBN-13: 978-1456414184

# Acknowledgements

To God: Thank you so much for continuing to allow me to write for you. The words of wisdom that you give me from Heaven are priceless and I am honored to share them with your people. Your love is greater than anything I've ever known. Thank you for saving me and putting me on such a great path. Thank you for saving my children. And I love you with all my heart.

To President Obama: You don't know me and I didn't vote for you. I am a republican and don't believe in many of the same things you do. You came to lead this country at a critical time. And I just want you to know I support you and am praying for you. Although I was once your greatest critic, God showed me you were meant to be our leader for this moment. And He will be implementing big changes through your administration. Please continue to help and guide this great country. And know that you are in our prayers. Regardless of what you believe, know that your creator loves you. And He created you to be where you are today.

To my children. All of you are so special to me. I couldn't have finished any writing without you standing by my side and encouraging me every step of the way. As children of a writer and student and coach and all the other things I do, you can sometimes be on the backburner. But you have never complained and have always pushed me to work harder and believe further. Without you my writing would have no meaning. Without the tireless late nights and crazy chance meetings I dragged you to in the hope that some day someone somewhere would believe in me, I wouldn't be where I am today. You held me up when the entire world was dragging me down. I know I live for you but you have taught me how to live for myself by reaching higher for the things that I once never thought I could have. You have helped make all my dreams come true. Thank you for all you do. I am honored to be your mother and can't wait to see what the future brings!

### NOT YOUR TYPICAL FOREWARD...
### BUT NOT YOUR TYPICAL BOOK, EITHER
### *(my comments are in the italics in parenthesis).*

"I have been a Christian for the past thirty years and have spent approximately forty-thousand hours in the study of His truths. I have written many articles about the church and other Christian topics and for the last ten years or also so for distribution. Commenting on the word of God I do not want to even imply making a contradiction, and when writing Bible commentary one must be aware that there are rules of interpretation that must be followed. You mention that God told you not to go to church *(because He wanted me to help the people who don't go to church-kinda hard to find them in the church when they **aren't there**).* This contradicts Heb 10:25 *(this scripture does not refer to the church building)* and you will probably respond with the unscriptural notion of God's spoken words trumps God's written words. You undoubtedly were taught this via TV preaching by one of the many false prophets that use this media *(right, because I am not a Bible student at a Christian college and you have ESP-it is scriptural and actually found in the book of Hebrews...the book you just quoted above).* TV preachers deny many Bible verses while also confusing many others resulting in many people being confused as to God's truth. See Peter's teaching of verse 2Pet 1:19-21. We have a more sure way than prophecy (speaking) that being the written word, verse Act 17:11, we have no way of determining truth except for using the Bible as our only benchmark to measure all things, all that is truth with agree. I could list more of where you have been misguided in your understanding of the Bible and Christianity but as with most people that receive their teaching from the TV you will probably reject this Godly council *(no, I reject your Ungodly council).* your teachings are filled with more error than truth and your view of Christianity as you described it, is not Christianity at all."

*Dear Sir: you can stick your comments where the sun don't shine and if you really think you are right, why don't you prove it? Die and let me know if God wanted me to listen to His voice or ignore Him. Let me know if God wanted me to sit in church and play with all the other church people or if he wanted me to step out in the real world and help real people. And while you're at it…oh, wait…you'll be dead so never mind. Your opinion won't matter any more. People like you are why this entire planet is perishing. God loves all His children and He says in His word His sheep hear his voice…you seem to be stuck on your own holiness which is probably why you can't hear His voice at all. I pray that you learn to listen to Him. And have a nice day*☺

The writer wishes to remain anonymous (that is a smart call!

# Introduction

The time for another book has come. As I type on my keyboard and I begin to write, I can't help but reflect on the length of time it took me to finish this one. I have been wrestling for years about this subject matter. It is not an easy one to write about and revealing many of the things I am about to in this book may mean the end of my "Christian" reputation. You can read from the forward I enclosed the type of thinking and opinions that I am up against.

I searched diligently for books that could help me with my sources, but realized after meticulous, long days of hunting that non-taxation of the church is more of an underground subject and I found very few publications that I could study for my research. It seems everyone wants to write a book about prayer, or worship, or salvation, but bring up churches and taxes and most of the authors of the past probably tucked their tail between their legs and ran the other way. And I understand. Since I began writing the very first chapter, my entire world has changed. I no longer attend the same church, run the same ministry, and have the same Christian friends. This was not by my choice, and I certainly was content with what I had before. These things changed because almost everyone in my life gave up on me. They turned their back, walked away, or just kicked me out. There are only a few precious friends left in my life that have stuck by my side. They know who they are and I thank them from the bottom of my heart.

When Jesus walked the Earth almost 2,000 years ago, he took the church by storm. He brought a heaven-sent butt whooping into the church and had some of his most heated debates with the people running it. These people asked Jesus about the validity of the things they were practicing in the church, and had some really great questions. Every time he answered their questions he told the people they were wrong to think and act the way they did. But they didn't do anything about it because nothing changed. Nothing at all has changed in the church regarding many of the items Jesus taught about. Since Jesus was God's son, he was doing exactly what God sent him to do. Seems like they didn't get the message 2000 years ago. And now God is trying to get the same message out there again.

As a writer, I am not a perfect person. And in no way do I wish to build myself up in this book. I have a long history of avoiding God and going my own way. So even in the midst of writing this I have stumbled and fallen short in my own trials. We are not perfect people. We are simply people called to a higher purpose than what we are doing here on Earth. And I hope that through reading this book, you find your higher purpose and begin to live out that precious calling in your own life.

So what is "Poligion"? It's politics and religion in the same subject. Jesus spoke about poligion and it was the only subject that brought him to anger. Don't believe me? It's right here in scripture…

Matthew 21:13 (NIV))

*"It is written," he (Jesus) said to them, " 'My house will be called a house of prayer, 'but you are making it a 'den of robbers."*

Prayer and robbers. Right? Religion and politics. But let's assume here that maybe religion isn't all right and politics isn't all wrong. Let's bring religion from its' 'holier than thou' place above us all and bring it down to earth and let's pull politics up out of the lowest and dirtiest ditches. Let's bring the two on the same level and address this issue presuming one isn't better than the other. Let's talk poligion…

I am about to delve into some serious subject matter. And many people will claim that I wrote this book just to make money and they will try to convince you that I am full of it. And yes, while I must admit I am full of it in many areas of my life, I did not sit around my house and try to stir up trouble for myself. I didn't ask for the task of bringing this message to you. And boy do I wish that just for ONCE my writing was about me. If it was about me, however, it wouldn't be a very big message, would it? No, this book isn't about me at all. This book is about YOU. All of you. I don't know why God chose me. I assume it is because I have a big mouth and an even bigger attitude. But I am simply the messenger in this book and the instrument that God used to get this message out to you.

I hope that after you read this book you will gain a better understanding of taxation and the church. If you are a pastor, missionary, or serve on a church staff, I hope you will fall on your knees and take this issue up with God, not the press. If it is really God who you pray to, He will let you know the truth. And if you are one of my devoted readers or a brand new one, I want to say thank you to you for reading my book and request that you pass this book on to someone you think may enjoy it. I have not written this book to hurt anyone. I am simply writing the truth. We live our lives searching for answers and trying to find the truth...all of us. So when we find it we have an obligation to tell others. That is why I wrote this book.

Looking back, I know it would have been easier to stop writing this book and forget it, maybe write a more 'comfortable' or less 'offensive' book. As my life was literally falling apart all around me, I could have just gave up and quit on this book like my old friends and ministry partners quit on me. But being a true servant is serving in all areas-even in the ones that hurt the most.

*I'd like to take a moment to recognize the authors of the resources I cited in this book. I wish to give honor where honor is due. They are the writers who did the hard work. I just analyzed their work and found ways to fit it into this book. The real heroes are the pioneers who began this research about non-taxation and the church. The ones who began the fight that I am now continuing.*

*And I thank them all for their dedication and perseverance.*

**Matthew 21:13 (New International Version, ©2010)**

*"It is written," he said to them, "'My house will be called a house of prayer,' but you are making it 'a den of robbers.'"*

# POLIGION

## Table of Contents

# CHAPTER 1

## RELIGION IS BIG BUSINESS

### *The conspiracy*

I have been a work in progress…a big one. God rescued me from a deep pit and has been repeatedly throwing me in the refining fire ever since. Often times I have no idea what He is trying to do with me, but I keep going and going and going. So when God birthed a successful single parents ministry in my life out of nothing, I had no idea how far we were going to go. Or how many lives we had the potential to change. The only thing I knew was I was supposed to help bring 25 rambunctious kids and their parents to South Africa for our first missions trip. I had never flown in a plane before and I hate bugs so the last place I wanted to end up was in South Africa. But the kids there touched my heart. I knew we needed to go help them. We needed a lot of money to make the trip. And I was ready to open my first business account.

"And what is your business?" the lady behind the desk at the bank asked me. She stopped typing and looked up from her computer.

"A children's ministry." I handed her my business card and smiled. "We have a sports ministry, perform skits at outreaches, have a street ministr….." I went on as I continued to impress myself. I told her I needed to open the account to send my daughter Jessica to South Africa. Jessica was my Overseas Missions Director and was eager for her first mission's trip.

The lady asked if I had a 501C3 certificate for non-profit. I took a deep breath in and smiled at her. This was the moment. The grand moment where I could change the world. I just knew it. My answer here was going to start something great…

"No. I will pay my taxes." I must admit that at this moment I felt rather righteous. I am sure that was not God's intention at all in this scenario. And I was very surprised at the woman's reaction, or shall I write *lack* of reaction to my answer. She obviously wasn't as impressed with me as I was.

"Oh. Okay." And that was all she said.

I paused for a brief moment. "Do you need anything else from me?" I wondered if she had heard what I said about paying my taxes. She kept typing at her computer and shook her head "no". It is really hard to feel righteous when it seems no one is even paying attention.

Apparently when you read the stories in the bible, you get the edited version of the lives of people. The trial comes, the wait begins, and then shortly after, the miracle happens. Sure, usually the scriptures read "100 years after" or "three generations had passed" but they seem to get their miracle on the very next paragraph. This is definitely not the speed that my miracle unfolded.

I expected lightning to strike, balloons to fall down from above, or the lady to leap over the counter and shake my hand. At the very least she could've called others over to hear my story. However this was no moment of bliss, and I wondered why God had told me to do such a thing.

The weeks that followed were anything but glorious. My entire life seemed to be teetering on the edge of sanity as everything was falling apart. Friends were being taken out of my life left and right. People who I had known for years seemed to avoid me like I had the plague. I had basically been driven out of my church (in a gracious way of course) and I spent most Sundays sitting with my kids on my bedroom floor making up our own children's church service. I felt like a foreigner in the house of God. And I was.

Then my daughter's first mission trip to South Africa fell through and she moved to the other side of the country. My youngest child had surgery to correct a horrible case of sleep apnea, my 10 year old began his first of many grand maul seizures and was diagnosed with epilepsy, my school grades were plummeting, and I went through my own series of tests to investigate an enlarged (but it turns out healthy) heart. To top it all off, some of my friends in ministry thought I was crazy. They continued to try to convince me to apply for non-profit status. I refused. And they stopped returning my calls.

So here I am, the proud owner of a ministry, sowing my money in and receiving very little financial support from anyone else to help with the expenses. I am arguing with many people about my decision to not file for non-profit status, and single mother-hood is putting a great financial burden on my shoulders in addition to the money I was spending for the children's ministry. Then I got a letter from my bank informing me that my ministry account was overdrawn, hit with overdraft fees, and being charged an additional daily fee until I could come in and pay on it. The bank wouldn't even let me close the account to avoid the daily fee and pay it off in increments even though I had two other accounts and had been a customer for several years. So I was tired, weary, broke, and wondered if I missed God somewhere along the way.

As I had so many times before, I lay in my bed and stared at the ceiling to talk to God. I was very confused and hurt. I didn't understand why God had told me to leave my career and all that I had been working towards to follow Him and His ways. I mean, what was He thinking? Leave money, my comfortable life and secure but turbulent marriage to basically live in the poor house as a single mother and follow God into the unknown? I really needed to find out what God wanted me to do. So I began to pray. The prayer was a great one-I was complaining, and begging, and protesting, but it didn't seem like He was even paying attention to me. "Come on God, where are you? I am so confused" I yelled. Nothing. Silence. I recalled the day's events and wondered if I had done anything to make God made at me. A few cuss words, I guess. Well, maybe more than a few...but *Why would he just ignore me?* I took a deep breath and stopped speaking. I opened my bible and began turning the pages. I guess this was His point to get a word in because something happened. It was revelation from heaven; a message that God spoke to me in the middle of my bedroom in the silence of the night. When He told me my jaw dropped and my eyes widened. Like a giant light bulb, something went off in my head: a spark of new life. "It's not in the bible."

WHAT?

"NON PROFIT MINISTRY-IT'S NOT IN THE BIBLE". He said it again, very clearly. And then He didn't say another word. I fell asleep that night with many questions running through my head. The word that God spoke to me absolutely blew my mind. Was that God? Or was it me? I wondered if I had heard it right. When I woke, I felt an urgency to investigate and began to study God's word and the Internet (two vital survival tools in today's world). I was looking for some kind of clue that would give me insight into the subject of non-profit ministry. I searched. And searched. And searched. And I found some intriguing answers.

What is a 501C3 corporation?

"A 501(c) organization is an American tax-exempt, nonprofit corporation or association. Section 501(c) of the United States Internal Revenue Code (26 U.S.C. § 501(c)), provides that 28 types of nonprofit organizations are exempt from some federal income taxes"

"501(c)(3) exemptions apply to corporations, and any community chest, fund, or foundation, organized and operated exclusively for religious, charitable, scientific, testing for public safety, literary, educational purposes, to foster national or international amateur sports competition, promote the arts, or for the prevention of cruelty to children or animals." (Wikipedia.com)

It turns out that getting your 501c3 is not that difficult of a task. Fill out the paperwork and you are well on your way. You can even download the forms off the Internet. Anyone can obtain non-profit status for a variety of businesses for as low as $300. There are many ways to become a non-profit. The web is cluttered with tons of sites dedicated to helping ministries and mission organizations obtain their 501C3, and most charge a nominal fee. There are also many lawyers turning a profit in the non-profit world for those people who feel more comfortable having someone else fill out the paperwork for them. But tax exemption for churches is not in the Bible. It is not a commandment that God ordained. It is not a rule that Jesus spoke. It is not engraved in stone making an 11<sup>th</sup> commandment. Non-profit ministry is not in the Bible.

So what? Big deal, right? Actually it is a big deal. And when I began researching this subject, I did not expect to find out what I did and I definitely didn't plan to write an entire book about it. I expected a few things to be out of whack, but once I continued my research and compared and verified sources, I was shocked. I am by nature a lazy and procrastinating person, often waiting till the very last minute to work on college papers and research reports. And my recliner can certainly verify that (well, if it could talk). So what was compelling me to move forward and work so hard on this book? The truth. Simply put…the truth.

So what is the truth? As a country we have put ourselves in a serious tax deficit by blatantly disobeying the word of God. You know the book that people can sometimes hold over your head and condemn you with? That book with all the rules and stories on how we are supposed to live? Yep. It's in the same book. The Bible that is being used by churches all across America instructs us that we must pay our taxes. Even the church. But we blindly set up a system that made 'sense' to help the church and ministries in their quest to honor God but in turn brought dishonor to Him. Because we never checked it out. We never investigated it. Now we as a nation have made it a habit to operate these businesses under a tax-exempt certificate so that most people are completely unaware of the real issue-that it's against the Word of God. Satan has set us up and is laughing his hot steamy butt off at us from his cozy place in Hell. Seriously. He helped make it almost automatic for countless churches and ministries across the nation to go against the word of God. Rendering them virtually helpless in these crucial days where we need God more than ever. These churches have disobeyed God and caused imminent destruction for their organization.

How serious of a tax deficit? A big one. There is a huge amount of taxes that aren't being paid by churches and other non-profits. And the American people absorb the cost of non-profits without even realizing it. They go to church and give their money and time to an organization that is not paying taxes and is actually putting their tax responsibility back on the American people-the same ones that are already paying for them to stay in business. In addition, this tax loss creates the need to raise taxes in other areas and cut budgets of local governments in all 50 states. Why didn't we address the issue when we were fighting our way out of the economic toilet a few years ago? Could this had been the start of a real solution?

I had to get more information on the subject matter because my head was cluttered with questions. So I went out and surveyed the American people. I think Americans are so cool. Certainly, they knew about this, right?

THE POLL….

1. Do you go to church?
2. Do you give them money?
3. Do you volunteer?
4. Did you know that churches and ministries don't pay taxes?
5. Do you know what the bible says about this?
6. How much revenue is the government losing yearly to church based non-profits?

Although many people I surveyed regularly attended church, they admitted they were unaware of what the bible specifically states about non-profit ministries. Everyone I interviewed knew that churches do not pay their taxes, which sparked a fairly heated discussion with a handful of them. One gentleman claimed the reason he left the church was because he felt manipulated by the entire tithing system, stating he lost his home while he was still giving faithfully. He felt the whole thing was a big scam. After hearing his heart-warming story, I had to agree with him. He was definitely duped by a church that had manipulated the word of God for their gain and never thought about his. And the church that did this didn't realize they were doing anything wrong at all. So even the church was being fooled.

Another gentleman gave me his opinion for about 30 minutes straight. I think I prayed more with him because I wanted God to send him away. But apparently I needed to listen to what he was saying because I did not get my wish. This guy told me he didn't understand why so many ministries out there claim to believe God for their prosperity, but then ask everyone else for money. And to top it off, the church is telling us to believe God for money, not people. Like, 'give us your money and trust God' but 'we won't trust God for our money, we will peddle you for it'. Hmm…never heard that sermon. And he had a great point. If these ministries really believed God, then they should take their own advice and ask God for money to support their business, not the American people. And these churches should quit telling people where to give their money. Isn't that God's job to tell us where to give our money anyways? Since He has the big ultimate plan and knows exactly where it needs to go?

I went back inside my house after a long and grueling day on the survey trail and embarked on a search to find these answers for myself. I had just discovered a new perspective on this subject after speaking with all the people out on the street. I was eager to look at this from a new angle. And I found some shocking answers to my questions.

According to an article written by Austin Cline at atheist.about.com, it is estimated that churches and religious organizations own up to 25% of the land in this country that amounts to approximately $100 billion of lost tax revenue (about.atheist.com). When you crunch all the numbers and total the tax revenue lost by these non-profits, it is fair to estimate that the average family may pay up to $1000.00 extra every year to absorb this tax loss. So that

'10%' you pay to the church is actually being taken from you off the other end as well…in the form of paying more taxes. I know that $1000.00 doesn't seem like a lot. But it adds up. In ten years it's $10,000.00. I don't want to pay money for someone else's slack. I think we have enough of that kind of taxpaying in this country. Don't you agree?

But don't these non-profits help the government? Don't churches help maintain a higher quality of life for Americans?

Time to go to the polls again…

1. How many churches have you attended in your life?
2. Did you ever get any help from these places?
3. Have you ever been turned away for help?
4. Were you asked to give money?  How often?

According to my reliable 'street sources' in Clearwater, FL, the local churches are really dropping the ball, especially when it comes to helping the American people. Many had been to churches over the past year to get help paying small bills and were turned away. At one church in particular, the woman was actually told by a staff member that the staff took pay cuts and had to cut out the entire benevolence fund they had sustained in their ministry for over 20 years!  But that same church in the same year was able to build a multi-million dollar facility to house their services and hold special Christian events. To this day they are continuing to serve their members and actively trying to recruit new ones by regularly hosting these events. But leaving the true heart of God outside their doors with the rest of the people who need real help- not another business to give to.

Others had been asked to give money two times every service, and were told the only way they were qualified to receive healing was to tithe into the ministry. You see this a lot on the television. After watching an entire day of television evangelism (during some programs I had to stop myself from vomiting and others I had to stop myself from throwing things at the t.v...) I counted how many ministries requested financial gifts from their viewers. It was an easy enough number to figure out, even without using my mad math skills...because it was 100%. For these ministries, well, I don't know who or what they were having faith in to receive their income...but you can probably come to your own conclusion.

One woman in particular was very upset. When I interviewed her she recalled the day her pastor said that the church was where you pay your 10% to God, and it was wrong to split up your tithe between your church and missions. In other words, she was being scolded because she had a heart to give to orphans in the far reaches of the world and used some of her tithe to support ministries there. And this was a single mother of 6 kids! She no longer attends that church and has no plans to return.

DISCLAIMER!!! "There are some great biblically sound churches and ministries out there that seem to be helping people. And while writing this book, I found one myself and now attend it. But the largest percentage of people I interviewed had not been to those churches".

So it seems to me that many people believe in God, but get turned away from the very churches God sends them to for help. Why have we decided that giving to God is giving to church? Is church God? Why does every single ministry feel compelled to ask for money from the American people and ask for tax relief from the government as soon as they open their doors?

I really didn't understand. In my opinion, it's a real shady way to run a business and a real bad way to represent God.

I have never thought of myself as a person worthy enough to do anything for anyone else. I have certainly messed up my own life so badly that I never want to relive any part of my past. But even I can see with all my huge faults and all my past mistakes that this looks like a great big rat.

Why should we volunteer and give our money to an organization that is taking from our government? In looking for more answers, I decided to check out this subject in the Bible. Maybe God has the answer…

Matthew 22:15-17 (NIV)

*"Then the Pharisees went out and laid plans to trap him in his words. They sent their disciples to him along with*

*the Herodians. "Teacher," they said, "we know you are a man of integrity and that you teach the way of God in accordance with the truth. You aren't swayed by men, because you pay no attention to who they are. Tell us then, what is your opinion? Is it right to pay taxes to Caesar or not?"*

Matthew 22:19-21

*Show me the coin used for paying the tax." They brought him a denarius, and he asked them, "Whose portrait is this? And whose inscription?"*

*"Caesar's," they replied.*

*Then he said to them, "Give to Caesar what is Caesar's, and to God what is God's."*

Okay, so that means I pay my money to the person or organization inscribed on it and give myself (Genesis 1: 27 *God created mankind in his own image, in the image of God he created them*) to God since His image is stamped on me. Simple enough. This means we must all pay our taxes because money is owed to the people who own it. There is no exception to the rule and there is no mention of churches getting exempt from this rule-at least Jesus the son of God didn't say it. Our government owns and runs our money so we pay it to them. But why do many churches and ministries get out of paying taxes in the first place? Especially when it is against the word of God? Maybe there is a scripture that can explain this.

Ezra 7 mentions taxes but contradicts the passage in Matthew. I have to enclose it because I am responsible to present both sides here...

*"You are also to know that you have no authority to impose taxes, tribute or duty on any of the priests, Levites, singers, gatekeepers, temple servants or other workers at this house of God. And I wouldn't even be writing this if it wasn't going to help us all in the long run."*

Okay. What's the difference then? A big one. Jesus, the Son of God spoke the words in Matthew. King Artaxerxes of Persia wrote the letter that is written in Ezra. He wrote it to a believer-a Jewish scribe. The "president" of that nation wrote it to a Jewish believer. And Artaxerxes was no angel. He was the son of Xerxes the previous king but got the throne appointed to him by his father's murderer, Artabanus. What makes Artaxerxes even more awesome is the fact that after he took the throne, he murdered his older brother Darius, and was probably the murderer of his other brother Hystaspes (netbible.org). He killed his family just to get and keep the position as King. I wouldn't believe a single word that came out of that murderer's mouth. He certainly wasn't hearing from God because the only force active in his life was Satan. King Artaxerxes was the king of selfishness. I think it's wise to stick to what Jesus said and bring the King's wisdom to the same fate as the rest of his family was brought to...by killing it.

But how did that get in the Bible? Only God can answer that one. Maybe He put it in there so I could put it in this book and help save the world (alright maybe not but you know it would be a good idea to me anyways). God intended the Bible to be a living and breathing book. A book that we can use to help us understand how to live better and help us understand more about His character and attributes (Bruce). Although the Bible is God-breathed, it was edited and translated by man. And many books weren't even included in the finished scriptures we use today. I wonder if those books had anything else to say about taxes and the church...but let's move on.

Another scripture about taxes we find in Romans

Romans 13:5-7 (NIV)

*Therefore, it is necessary to submit to the authorities, not only because of possible punishment but also because of conscience. This is also why you pay taxes, for the authorities are God's servants, who give their full time to governing. Give everyone what you owe him: If you owe taxes, pay taxes; if revenue, then revenue; if respect, then respect; if honor, then honor.*

This further solidifies the point I am presenting in this book. God is telling us that the people who serve in government are His servants. And we should pay our taxes to help them. It is right there in the Bible. In black and white. The very Bible that churches all over America read from. How can churches just skip over that scripture when they are writing their budgets? Don't they read the same Bible I do? Don't they read the same Bible you do?

Even Jesus paid his taxes. Yes he did. It's in the book of Matthew…In chapter 17-

*After Jesus and his disciples arrived in Capernaum, the collectors of the two-drachma temple tax came to Peter and asked, "Doesn't your teacher pay the temple tax?"*

*25 "Yes, he does," he replied.*

### *FURTHER IN THE VERSE-*

*Jesus said to him. 27 "But so that we may not cause offense, go to the lake and throw out your line. Take the first fish you catch; open its mouth and you will find a four-drachma coin. Take it and give it to them for my tax and yours."*

Jesus paid his taxes. JESUS. However, many churches and ministries today aren't paying taxes and as a result are applying a great deal of pressure on the government to raise taxes and cut budgets. The non-profit ministries are actually doing more harm than good, and could be responsible for some of the financial corruption that is running rampant through this country. It is throwing the entire system in a downward spiral and is clearly against the written word of God. The book that churches claim to believe above all other books.

God is bigger than taxes and to serve Him doesn't mean you should get out of your tax responsibility. God makes it clear in His scriptures that we should pay our taxes to help our government. Period. If anything goes against the written word of God and is not commanded by God himself, then it is not His word.

It is not the President's fault, the war's fault, or the oil companies' fault that this nation is in chaos. It is simply God doing exactly what He says in His word. He is trying to get our attention. God made everything and He knows how to fix anything.

Matthew 15:13 (NIV)

### *"Every plant that my heavenly Father has not planted will be pulled up by the root"*

God wants to bring His people to Him, not church. He knows in the dark corners of the homes in America what is ultimately keeping His people away from Him. It's not the body piercings, the crazy clothing and hair, alcohol addiction, or drugs and sex that are alienating the people from God. Jesus went to help all those people. He helped the homeless and hurting, the drug addicts and the prostitutes. God specializes in taking messy lives and fixing them. I know that firsthand because He fixed mine. But if you investigate the scriptures, it was in the church at the moneychangers' tables that Jesus wanted to turn the tables upside down. It was there that He was brought to a passion that made him do the only aggressive act written about in the entire New Testament. He was very angry because the church was stealing from the people, and cheating God. Nowhere in the Bible is there another moment that Jesus was brought to an aggression like this.

Mark 11:15-16 (KJV)

*And they came to Jerusalem, and Jesus went into the temple and began to cast out them that sold and bought in the temple, and overthrew the tables of the moneychangers, and the seats of them that sold doves*;

John 2:13-15 (NIV)

*When it was almost time for the Jewish Passover, Jesus went up to Jerusalem. In the temple courts he found men selling cattle sheep and doves, and others sitting at tables exchanging money. So he made a whip out of cords, and drove all from the temple area, both sheep and cattle; he scattered the coins of the moneychangers and overturned their tables.*

Jesus made a whip to drive everyone out of the temple. He actually made a weapon to inflict fear and make people listen...He did other things too that went against the churches laws and traditions. Jesus healed (worked) on the Sabbath day sending us a message that it is best to do God's work every day, even if it means doing it on Sunday. Jesus praised a widow for giving a few cents to the church over all the money that the rich were giving sending us a message that it is not the amount of money that we give but it is the giving of our heart and our faith in God that is priceless. And he stated that 'I am able to destroy the temple of God and rebuild it in three days.' (Matthew 26:61) sending us the message that the new church is not the building and we do not have to go anywhere to get to God-we only need to rely on the finished work of Christ. I can write that again...Jesus sent us the message that the new church is NOT the building and we DO NOT have to go anywhere to get to God-we only need to rely on the FINISHED WORK of Christ. Jesus changed many things for us when he came and taught. He made sure to let us know that paying taxes is a part of church responsibility to God. And he sent that message on the tail end of a nasty handmade whip. Jesus opened a big old can of whoop on the church!

# CHAPTER 2

## WHAT WOULD JESUS DO?

### *He would pay his taxes*

A gentleman from the church that I used to belong to stopped by my house to pay a quick visit. It was surprising to me that I was visited as I had left the church 6 months before and not even a phone call was made to check up on me. I figured my absence from that church made many people grateful that I was gone. I wasn't considered one of the "normal" members of the congregation. I had a big mouth and an even bigger heart and I was not afraid to use them. When I would see something that didn't look right, I'd speak up. And there were plenty of things at that church to speak up about because many things weren't right.

When I saw him at the door I rolled my eyes and sighed. I asked God to make him go away but apparently God wasn't listening to me because he didn't vanish into thin air. I waited for a moment to give God extra time but he was still standing there in the same place waiting for me to answer. He wasn't going anywhere. So I opened the door and invited him into my home. He shook my hand and we sat down to have a little talk.

I gave him the summary of my life over the past 6 months since my departure from the church. He told me a little about what he'd been up to, and then he asked the inevitable question…"are you going to church now?"

"Nope. I bounce from church to church. I get my sermons from the television and internet ministries, I hold my own church on the streets with kids, and I go to chapel at my college three days a week. The rest of the time I go where God tells me to and I spend time with people He tells me to spend time with. I'm right where God wants me." I figured that was enough church to shut him up. I really did not want to talk about church with him. He had always been one of those people that made the hairs stand up on the back of my neck. But I was not successful in shutting him up because he kept talking. And there went the hairs…

He said, "Well, you need to be rooted and grounded in church." *Great.* I thought. *Here we go.*

"I am rooted and grounded…in the Bible-God's word." I answered back.

"That's not good enough. You have to be in church."

I sighed and protested. "Look, if I was stuck in church on Sunday, I would miss all the opportunities to show people and tell people about God's love. God told me that the people He wanted me to help aren't in church on Sundays. And He's right. They're at the gym, the park, the grocery st…"

"You need to be in church." He interrupted.

And we continued to debate. Eventually, we got on the subject of money. He said that the people who had left the church and walked away from their financial responsibility to the building fund were the reason that the church was struggling with money. Apparently I wasn't the only member who got shooed out of that church. And now the church was reaping the benefits of kicking out all its money and help. I shook my head. "How are we held responsible for a building fund to a church? And who are we to say that the people who left aren't sowing seed into God's Kingdom, just at another place? God is the one who brings ministries up and puts them down, not people. Obviously the church has missed God somewhere and needs to go to Him to fix their finances, not the people. It says in God's word that we should pay our taxes. All of us."

"Well, all the churches are non-profit. That doesn't make any sense." He answered back.

"That's what God told me." I looked at him with determination in my eyes. He knew I meant business.

"We have to offer people a way to pay their tithe to God through the church. You just can't throw it up in the air and expect God to catch it. Besides, we gave $800,000.00 to overseas missions last year. We could not have done that if we had to pay taxes." He thought what he just said made perfect sense so I had to continue on. I have this annoying determination to always be right. Sometimes God can use it for good but other times I can go off on my own and forget all about God.

"God is bigger than taxes. And how do you know He wasn't prepared to give us 10 times that amount if we paid our taxes?"

He started to say something back but didn't know what to say. So he looked at me, got up from the couch, and turned to leave. I guess he'd had enough and I obviously wasn't budging from my point of view. I ushered him out the door and said goodbye. I was glad he left and went back to my computer to investigate this subject further by exploring church tax history. I typed the words in my Internet search and hit enter. And this is what I came up with…

On average the local government receives approximately 64 % of its general tax revenue from property taxes every year (Scott). Churches own a majority of untaxed property in America. The notion of tax exemption for church property is an old one that dates back to the beginning of bible records. Genesis 47:26 records Pharaoh exempting the priests' land from taxation, and Ezra 7:14 indicates that none of the priests, Levites, singers, porters or ministers of the house of God were to be charged tax. In the days of Roman Emperor Constantine, church buildings and the land surrounding them were exempt. Centuries later, European countries continued the tradition of tax exemption, primarily because the church regularly controlled the state. In other words, the church was the government in those days. That is definitely not the way the United States has set up its government.

In the U.S., property tax exemption for churches was birthed in colonial days. In 1802, for example, the Seventh Congress exempted religious bodies from real estate taxes. On the state level, specific exemptions from property taxes for churches were established in Virginia in 1777, New York in 1799, and the city of Washington in 1802. "The exemptions for churches have continued uninterrupted to the present day," Justice William 3. Brennan has said. 'They are in force in all 50 states" (quoted by Leo Pfeffer in "The Special Constitutional Status of Religion," Taxation and the Free Exercise of Religion, edited by John Baker [Baptist Joint Committee on Public Affairs, 1978], p. 711).

In a federal court hearing in 1972 in the case of Christian Echoes National Ministry, Inc. v. U.S., the Tenth Circuit Court ruled, "tax exemption is a privilege, a matter of grace rather than a right." (IRS.gov)

Obviously this subject has been a controversial one for centuries. So what is the big deal and why all the fuss?

Let me explain further. Tax exemptions and tax deductibility are both forms of subsidy that are administered through the tax system. A tax exemption has much the same effect as a cash grant to the organization of the amount of tax it would have to pay on its income. How much cash are we talking about here? A lot. Sole proprietorships ring in at a 13.3 percent rate, small partnerships face 23.6 percent, small C corporations pay 17.5 percent, and small S corporations face a whopping 26.9 percent. This is only the tax applied to the income of the business and does not include the taxes companies pay on goods, services, and property. (biztaxlaw)

If tax exemption is a form of subsidy, then church property tax exemption is a clear violation of the establishment clause of the First Amendment. Gotta love America. Another brilliant opportunity to tromp all over the Bill of Rights for the "good" of the people.

"The First Amendment to the United States Constitution is part of the Bill of Rights. The amendment prohibits the making of any law "respecting an establishment of religion", impeding the free exercise of religion, infringing on the freedom of speech, infringing on the freedom of the press, interfering with the right to peaceably assemble or prohibiting the petitioning for a governmental redress of grievances. Originally, the First Amendment only applied to the Congress. However, in the 20th century, the Supreme Court held that the Due Process Clause of the Fourteenth Amendment applies the First Amendment to each state, including any local government" (wikipedia).

If you dig a little further back to a publication called "The Federalist Papers", in Federalist # 12 written by Alexander Hamilton titled "The Utility of the Union in Respect to Revenue", you uncover more evidence about the importance of tax revenue in the United States of America...

"A nation cannot long exist without revenues. Destitute of this essential support, it must resign its independence, and sink into the degraded condition of a province. This is an extremity to which no government will of choice accede. Revenue, therefore, must be had at all events. In this country, if the principal part be not drawn from commerce, it must fall with oppressive weight upon land (founding fathers)."

These "Federalist Papers" were written in the years 1787 and 1788 and published in several New York newspapers. The authors of The Federalist wanted to shape future interpretations of the U.S. Constitution. Alexander Hamilton was the largest contributor to The Federalist Papers and he signed the original U.S. Constitution.

So why is there tax exemption for churches if it is against God's word and the laws of this great nation?

Some claim that tax exemption for churches has helped a pluralistic (existence of different groups within a society) society in which a broad range of religious perspectives can flourish. They state that such pluralism (a term used to describe the acceptance of all religious paths as equally valid, promoting coexistence) (wikipedia) safeguards against extremism and should be maintained. However the church of scientology, which many would argue is an extreme religion, has benefited from non-profit status. After an extensive study performed by the IRS, they decided in October 1993 that the Church of Scientology should be recognized as a non-profit charitable organization, with full tax-exempt status in the United States. They were allowed to obtain their 501c3 because they are considered a church and other churches have it. This decision was made because way back in 1894 Congress passed a law granting religious tax exemption to some organizations (Jacobson). So did tax exemption really help in this case or did it instead support extremism?

Others claim that levying property taxes upon churches would have the effect of closing the doors of thousands of small congregations that operate on a very tight budget. That many downtown churches would be forced out by the property taxes on their valuable land. Or so they claim this would happen. But even without paying taxes, churches of every denomination in cities across the nation have been closing.

Paying your taxes is part of God's plan for His people. Not paying taxes is actually against His word. So while you may be part of a great congregation that is growing and has an excellent marketing plan, you must ask yourself if the church you are attending is part of God's marketing plan or if they have one of their own. Simply put-if they pay their taxes they are part of God's marketing plan, but if they don't then they may or may not be. Which bring us to the next chapter.

# CHAPTER 3

## IS IT ALL CHURCHES?

*Don't bring the pitchfork and open*

*flames to your local church just yet!*

Is it all churches and ministries? Are they all supposed to be paying taxes? These were questions that I wondered about a lot while writing this book. It was hard to understand how things could have gotten so turned around and out of control. And I had seen several churches and ministry organizations that did well financially and seemed to help a great deal of people. So what was the catch? The loophole? Was there one?

The written word of God is the final authority on Earth except for one other source. This source is to be used with the Bible and often times will bring clarity to the highly debatable subjects that religious scholars have been discussing and arguing over for years.

What is it? It is the spoken word of God.

There are a handful of television preachers that I enjoy watching that seem to do well and are quite effective at helping others. These preachers have what I call "super-ministries". Not only do they pastor their own churches, they televise world-wide in several languages, author books that regularly grace the bestseller lists, give generously to overseas missions, and continue to experience growth in their ministry even when the economy has caused countless others to fold.

There are also great mission organizations that are experiencing growth. My good friends from South Africa have turned an entire village into a thriving and self-sustaining community, erecting a huge facility to house their church that was built debt free by the generous contributions of supporters and a local builder. They are also building homes for the orphans in the village and are digging a well to support a farm for the villagers to work. They are experiencing this growth because they too have heard from God about becoming a 501c3 and continue to receive His blessings unhindered by any cracks in the foundation of their ministry.

The point of this book is not to give a message that "all churches should pay their taxes." There are some ministries that prayed and waited to hear from God before they moved forward with the decision to become a 501c3. I know this because I have seen churches handle it both ways. However, on the flip side of the coin, virtually every church in America seems to be operating under a 501c3 certificate. And that is wrong. Even with the non-profit status, many religious organizations are closing their doors permanently. Countless other churches are being forced to make several budget cuts because they are building their ministry with a huge crack in the foundation. And they are doing this with your hard-earned dollars! So your taxes are helping businesses go broke at the average rate of $1000.00 out of your pocket every year.

God has a specific way that every church and ministry needs to operate and He has specific instructions on how to grow those organizations, including instructions on paying taxes. Even when you have great ideas and feel like your church/ministry will benefit from them, if it is not God's idea, it will be very difficult to see long term growth come from it.

There are two types of churches and religious organizations in the world today. But they appear to be the same type at first glance. Some run their churches and organizations like a business with money at the core of all their decisions. And the others run their churches and organizations like a ministry with God at the core of all their decisions. But the deception in those businesses is that they appear very similar. Both types can have great Bible studies and great sermons. They can both have good worship music and tons of small group ministries to service their members. Both can send out missionaries to the far reaches of the world and help with the global issues of poverty and AIDS. Both can have weekly prayer meetings and fellowship. But only one type is serving God. The other is serving money. The other type is serving money TAX FREE. What a deal, huh?

But don't taxpayers get a tax reduction for charitable contributions? For some people, this is a way to lower their tax liability. It can be a good idea and make a lot of sense to lower your taxes by giving to these organizations. But again, is this a way to fix the economy by reducing even more tax revenue the government receives? Or is it another way to encourage people to support these non-profits that are already getting a huge tax break and creating a serious tax deficit? Think about it…

# CHAPTER 4

## SO…WHO IS GOD?

### *'God'-simplified*

So who is God? And what does the Bible say about Him?

To the Buddhist, the Jew, the Muslim, the Christian, the Methodist, the Catholic, the Presbyterian, the Lutheran, and other religions He is love. Plain and simple, God is love.

1 John 4:8 (NIV)

**Whoever does not love does not know God,**

**because God is love.**

Deuteronomy 7:9-10 (NIV)

**Know therefore that the LORD your God is God; he is the faithful God, keeping his covenant of love to a thousand generations of those who love him and keep his commands.**

God does not have a religion. He does not favor any religion. God is love. He has a commandment of love with each one of His believers. It says the Bible that love is the greatest commandment and that love takes priority over all other commandments. God is serving others. God is unselfish. God is gracious. God is gentle, kind, and lovely.

God is not a prominent figure standing at the pulpit that knows the bible like the back of his hand. God is not found sitting in the front row of every church across America. Luke 20:46-47 (New Living Translation)

*"Beware of these teachers of religious law! For they like to parade around in flowing robes and love to receive respectful greetings as they walk in the marketplaces. And how they love the seats of honor in the synagogues and the head table at banquets. Yet they shamelessly cheat widows out of their property and then pretend to be pious by making long prayers in public."*

The longer and deeper I've gotten to know God, the more I've been brought to the realization that God is love. Period.

I built my home with peaceful Buddhists. I sat side by side with knowledgeable Jewish believers in a Bible study. I go to school with the best Christians I've ever met. I was raised as a Presbyterian and I have had great meals and fellowship with my Muslim neighbors. I even have had visits in my home by Satanists, Atheists, and Wickens and we discuss God. God is bigger than religion. He is not bound by any religion. He is everywhere. And He made everything. God is love.

Matthew 22:36-40 (KJV)

*Master, which is the great commandment in the law?*

*Jesus said unto him, Thou shalt love the Lord thy God with all thy heart, and with all thy soul, and with all thy mind.*

*This is the first and great commandment.*

*And the second is like unto it, Thou shalt love thy neighbour as thyself.*

*On these two commandments hang all the law and the prophets.*

Love is the first and greatest commandment. And love is also the second commandment. Loving God and loving your neighbor; these are the two commandments that we should all follow. These are the commandments that go before all other commandments. The commandment of LOVE.

But love doesn't stop there. Not only is it the first and greatest commandment, it is also our hidden power. Our power to get healed, our power to get delivered, and our power to get prosperity in life. Simply put love is the only thing you need to give and it's the only thing you need to get to have the life you've always wanted.

Ephesians 3:20

*Now to him who is able to do immeasurably more than all we ask or imagine, according to his power that is at work within us.*

If you want more love in your life, then you need to get closer to God. You need to get to know Him on a personal level. If you desire to get up close and personal with the creator of everything, if you long for solid inner peace and are striving to find your place in this world, allow God to live inside of you and get to know Him intimately so He can change your life. Allow God to change your life through His love. God didn't make you so that you would live a miserable life. He created you so that you could live a great life. He doesn't want you to be unhappy. He doesn't want you to be stressed out. God's plan was never to allow you to endure suffering without a way out.

What kind of life will you live? You will live a spectacular one. Better than anything you've ever dreamed. Once God sends His spirit to live inside you, a miraculous transformation will take place. You will be transformed by the renewing of your mind. Your thinking will change. Your view will change, your heart will change, and eventually your life will change. It is a slow process that can take several years to complete, but you will finally live the life you've always strived to get. And things will fall into place one by one as you walk out God's will for your life by walking in love.

How do you get God to send His spirit to live inside of you?  Just ask Him to send it.  Ask God to save you.  Receive salvation.

Acts 28:28 (NIV)

*Therefore I want you to know that God's salvation has been sent to the Gentiles, and they will listen!"*

It doesn't make a difference what religion you grew up following.  It doesn't matter if you're a Buddhist, Jew, Muslim, Catholic, Lutheran, Methodist, or Christian.  Receiving salvation doesn't qualify you to be a born-again Christian.  Receiving salvation doesn't force you into any religion.  You can keep the one you have.  All receiving salvation qualifies you for is to become a born-again BELIEVER.  It is the way to be reconciled through the blood of Jesus Christ to an eternal covenant with the Father.  Regardless of what religion you follow.  Receiving salvation simply redeems you from the curse and connects you with the promise.  You don't even have to go to church in a way to "keep it".  Once you receive it, it is yours as long as it is done with your heart.  And you are instantly given the gift of eternal life.

The Bible says we are saved by faith.  That it is a gift from God and can't be earned through good works.  We must hear and believe the gospel, which is the 'good news' of Jesus' death and resurrection. This is found in Ephesians 1:16-23

*I keep asking that the God of our Lord Jesus Christ, the glorious Father, may give you the Spirit of wisdom and revelation, so that you may know him better. I pray also that the eyes of your heart may be enlightened in order that you may know the hope to which he has called you, the riches of his glorious inheritance in the saints, and his incomparably great power for us who believe. That power is like the working of his mighty strength, which he exerted in Christ when he raised him from the dead and seated him at his right hand in the heavenly realms, far above all rule and authority, power and dominion, and every title that can be given, not only in the present age but also in the one to come. And God placed all things under his feet and appointed him to be head over everything for the church, which is his body, the fullness of him who fills everything in every way.*

Then we must fully trust and believe the Lord Jesus. This is found in Romans 1:16

*"I am not ashamed of the gospel, because it is the power of God for the salvation of everyone who believes: first for the Jew, then for the Gentile. For in the gospel a righteousness from God is revealed, a righteousness that is by faith from first to last, just as it is written: "The*

*righteous will live by faith."*

You must repent for your sins, and renew your mind about Christ. This is found in Acts 3:19

*Repent, then, and turn to God, so that your sins may be wiped out, that times of refreshing may come from the Lord,*

And confess with your mouth and believe in your heart that Jesus is Lord, died on the cross so that you could be forgiven of your sins, and that God raised him from the dead. This is found in Romans 10:9-10.

*That if you confess with your mouth, "Jesus is Lord," and believe in your heart that God raised him from the dead, you will be saved. For it is with your heart that you believe and are justified, and it is with your mouth that you confess and are saved.*

But even if you don't go step by step, you can still receive salvation. Just make the request. I only spoke two words to God when I received mine. I didn't own a Bible or have any friends who went to church. I got hives every time I heard or thought about church and definitely hadn't been to a service for quite some time. My mouth alone was bad enough to keep anyone around me out of heaven. And I was ready for help. So I recruited the only help left for me since I had pretty much pushed everyone else away. I cried up to the heavens and said "save me". I didn't even know what I was doing. I was backed up against a wall and was forced to make a decision I didn't want to make. And I needed help. I figured God existed, since we all had to come from something much greater than ourselves. Everything had to begin somewhere. So I made a decision to turn to Him for help. And it was those words I spoke that changed my entire life. God sees the true heart of all His children. And I was reaching out to Him from the bottom of mine.

God hears you when you call out to Him. And He is waiting for you to ask Him to help you. All of us know God in some capacity. He created us and when we ask Him to get involved in our life, it feels like the feeling you get when you return to your home after a long trip. You get rest, feel relaxed, and know you are right where you belong. Although you may feel like God has forgotten you, He has not. And God is waiting for the opportunity to intervene in your life. He created you so that you could live part of your life, build a great testimony in the process, and then get to the point where you have to turn to Him for help. Once that happens, God can get to work. I know that it seems cruel that He wouldn't just prevent all the bad stuff from happening to us but it is not. Joseph had to be thrown in a pit and sold into slavery to become 2$^{nd}$ in command of Egypt. So why wouldn't God need to throw us somewhere low so He could bring us much higher?

Your suffering, my suffering, is all part of a big huge plan He has to save the world. Your mistakes, my mistakes, all happened to work out for good in the end. So leave your past in the past and go to God for your future. He will transform your life and renew your mind by communicating with you through prayer and the words in the Bible, and then put you on the right path towards the life you were created to live. And that testimony you've been building through all your past mistakes He will use in your future so you can help others. Receive salvation and get to know God in a deeper and more intimate way. Allow Him to transform everything and bring you to the victory you've always longed to have!

Many people are afraid that they aren't qualified for God's love and help. Like they've done something unforgiveable and they couldn't possibly recover into a victorious life. Some are so deep in a pit that they gave up hope a long time ago and quit looking for a way out. I have one sentence, one phrase, one thing to write to you and I pray that it goes deep in your heart and sticks with you forever...

## YOU ARE NO SURPRISE TO GOD.

God created you. He created you with all your beauty and all your faults. He created you with your good points and your bad points. God says in His word we are all "beautifully and wonderfully made". He never said we are perfect. And just like pieces of a puzzle, we all fit together in a unique way and He created us all to be part of the puzzle to complete it. So come just as you are. And if there are any items that need fixing in your life, God will lead you to those things and take you through experiences that will change them. All you need to do is be available for those changes to take place. You are no surprise to God.

And there is nothing that you have done in your past that can separate you from coming to Him today. I succeeded in breaking all ten commandments before I asked Him for help. No, I didn't physically kill anyone but we commit murder just by thinking bad about someone else (holy crap-I am in BIG trouble on this one). I always want to do things completely and I never leave things unfinished. So sinning was very easy for me to do. And I did it well. I was among the worst of them. Trust me. Everything you have done in your past I have probably done or come close to doing.

You don't need to be perfect to come to God. You don't need to be sin-free to qualify for the good life. God wants you to have it. He has it waiting for you to get. And you are the only one stopping you from getting it.

Nothing you have done in your past disqualifies you for a glorious future with God. God loves you so much. He put something in you that is so special. He has the perfect plan for your life. And He wants you to find that plan by going to Him to get it.

Strap on the seatbelt and enjoy the ride. I know it's scary, like the first time you tried a roller coaster. You know there will be twists and turns, ups and downs. Sometimes you are going to feel great, other times you will have fear. There are times when you will know what is coming up but then there will be other times when you can't see the next turn. But with God, you will have a helper. You will have a co-passenger. And He will help you through those moments so you can come out of them unharmed. So jump in the seat. Recruit God to come with you and sit beside you on the roller coaster of life. Just do it.

# CHAPTER 5

## WHY DO WE NEED GOD?

### *Besides the whole 'eternal damnation' thing...*

Good question...let me expound. Since the right information is key to understanding God, I'd like to give you as much as I can in this chapter.

So many times I have been led the wrong way. I have turned the wrong direction and gone down the wrong path. For many years I thought that my bad luck and misfortunes were part of my own bad decision making. But they weren't...well, sort of. Yes, I made dumb decisions. Stupid mistakes. If God didn't love me unconditionally I would be dead or in jail for life right now. The information I am about to share with you is the truth. I do not have a church or business I am trying to fund through this book. I am not sharing this with you to peddle you for more money or trap you into giving to an organization. I have no ministry affiliations any more. All I want from you is your undivided attention for this chapter. I want you to understand what you are dealing with, what we are all dealing with. And most of all, I want you to realize that anything bad that is happening to you right now can be reversed.

Have you noticed an increase in bad weather-floods in some areas and droughts in others? Have you noticed an increase in financial troubles and a huge increase in the types of sicknesses that are sweeping across this country and affecting people regardless of how healthy they are? Corruption is prevalent in countless lives in all types of professions. Abuse is running rampant through this nation. Divorce rates are at an unbelievable high, even among groups proclaiming to be religious. Abortion and murder are taking more lives away than ever before. As a matter of fact we aborted many of the babies who were going to grow up and help sustain our social security fund. We were so busy defending our 'right to choose' that we lost sight of the big picture. Yes, we made the choice to kill them and now we are paying the price. Teenage pregnancy is at an all time high. This nation has opened day care centers in its public high schools to accommodate the massive number of teen mothers. And I could go on and on.

We need God because without Him, we are cursed. It says this in the bible.

Deuteronomy 28:13-30(TLB)

*If you will only listen and obey the commandments of the Lord your God that I am giving you today, he will make you the head and not the tail, and you shall always have the upper hand. But each of these blessings depends on your not turning aside in any way from the laws I have given you; and you must never worship other gods.*

*If you won't listen to the Lord your God and won't obey these laws I am giving you today, then all of these curses shall come upon you:*

*Curses in the city;*

*Curses in the fields;*

*Curses on your fruit and bread;*

*The curse of barren wombs;*

*Curses upon your crops;*

*Curse upon the fertility of your cattle and flocks;*

*Curses when you come in;*

*Curses when you go out.*

*For the Lord himself will send his personal curse upon you. You will be confused and a failure in everything you do, until at last you are destroyed because of the sin of forsaking him. He will send disease among you until you are destroyed from the face of the land which you are about to enter and possess. He will send tuberculosis, fever, infections, plague, and war. He will blight your crops, covering them with mildew. All these devastations shall pursue you until you perish.*

*The heavens above you will be as unyielding as bronze, and the earth beneath will be as iron. The land will become as dry as dust for lack of rain, and dust storms shall destroy you.*

*The Lord will cause you to be defeated by your enemies. You will march out to battle gloriously, but flee before your enemies in utter confusion; and you will be tossed to and fro among all the nations of the earth. Your dead bodies will be food to the birds and wild animals, and no one will be there to chase them away.*

*He will send upon you Egyptian boils, tumors, scurvy, and itch, for none of which will there be a remedy. He will send madness, blindness, fear, and panic upon you. You shall grope in the bright sunlight just as the blind man gropes in darkness. You shall not prosper in anything you do; you will be oppressed and robbed continually, and nothing will save you.*

*Someone else will marry your fiancée; someone else will live in the house you build; someone else will eat the fruit of the vineyard you plant.*

Do we have incurable disease in this country today? Homes that are being lost and businesses destroyed? Infidelity? Fear? Did we recently fight a war that we should not have suffered many casualties yet thousands of lives were lost?

What is happening in the world is not necessarily evidence of the end times. It is simply we as a nation being disobedient to God's laws and commandments, permanently keeping us from a blessed life and holding us under the curse: the curse that God placed on us thousands of years ago in the Garden of Eden. This curse is a direct result of our disobedience as a nation. It has been placed on us because of sin. And instead of looking to God for a way out, we have settled for talk shows and infomercials to tell us what we are supposed to do. We have settled for the human solution to a spiritual problem.

So what do we need to do? I am glad you asked. What we need to do does not require any extra money. It does not require a great deal of effort or time, or some 'ingenious' invention to fix all the bad. You don't need to read your horoscope or go to a palm reader to look into the future to fix it. There is no foolproof formula that we need to come up with to remedy these issues. We simply do not have the solution. So we cannot 'do' anything to fix it. We need to get with God and have Him fix it. He is the only one powerful enough to help us now. And to find His power we go to the Bible and search through His word.

The solution to the country's problems is found in the scriptures. This solution only takes a few minutes a day and it will completely change us all individually and as a nation and permanently hook us into the blessing. It is a three-step process that will stop the curse completely and fix the condition of your life forever. Don't you want that to happen in your own life? Aren't you fed up with coming close but always falling short of a blessed life?

Isn't it time to step into the future you were created to live?

The solution begins with a little thing called faith. Faith is step one.

Hebrews 11:1 (NIV)

*Now faith is being sure of what we hope for and certain of what we do not see.*

Hebrews 11:3- 12 (NIV)

*By faith we understand that the universe was formed at God's command, so that what is seen was not made out of what was visible.*

*By faith Abel offered God a better sacrifice than Cain did. By faith he was commended as a righteous man, when God spoke well of his offerings. And by faith he still speaks, even though he is dead.*

*By faith Enoch was taken from this life, so that he did not experience death; he could not be found, because God had taken him away. For before he was taken, he was commended as one who pleased God. And without faith it is impossible to please God, because anyone who comes to him must believe that he exists and that he rewards those who earnestly seek him.*

*By faith Noah, when warned about things not yet seen, in holy fear built an ark to save his family. By this faith he condemned the world and became heir of the righteousness that comes by faith.*

*By faith Abraham, when called to go to a place he would later receive as his inheritance, obeyed and went, even though he did not know where he was going. By faith he made his home in the promised-land like a stranger is a foreign country; he lived in tents, as did Isaac and Jacob, who were heirs with him of the same promise. For he was looking forward to the city with foundations, whose architect and builder is God.*

*By faith Abraham, even though he was past age-and Sarah herself was barren-was enabled to become a father because he considered him faithful who had made the promise. And so from this one man, and he as good as dead, came descendants as numerous as the stars in the sky and as countless as the sand on the seashore.*

These victories in the Bible occurred because of faith. And faith is having confidence in what you cannot see. You can pray all day and go to every church service in town. You can feed the homeless and orphans and give your entire life over to helping others. But if you don't have faith then you have nothing. Your prayers won't be answered, your work won't be honored, and your sacrifice won't be recognized. You can dress up and play church all day but God is never fooled. He sees your faith through the outward appearance. He is not impressed by your willingness to do 'good'. He is not fooled by your ability to recite the Bible. He doesn't care whether you are ordained as a minister or you live your life as a tattoo artist in the inner city. The only thing He is looking for…the only thing that makes God move is faith. The most important thing in the world is faith.

So how do you know what it is you are believing for? Especially if you can't see it? It is all in the Bible. The covenants of God and His inheritance He left for us are listed all over the scriptures. God's will and testament are in the Bible and the way you receive them is to enter into covenant with Him. And faith is the first step towards getting out from underneath the curse and becoming heirs to His promises.

The cross has two main pieces to it. A vertical piece and a horizontal piece. And there's a place where they intersect. We all live horizontally. If you go to the ocean and look as far as you can, you see the earth and the sky come together at a horizon. That is what we see and that is how we live. We live our lives making decisions based on what we can see. Horizontally. God gives us life vertically. He operates in a world we cannot see. The spiritual world is real and it is happening all around us. But it operates opposite of what we can see in the physical world. Vertically. And that is how He gets us to our victory-by leading us using a world we cannot see. So we need to have faith in what we cannot see. And that is why the cross has such significance in our lives. The cross is where the horizontal (or physical world) and the vertical (or spiritual) world intersect. Without faith in the cross-faith in Christ, we have nothing to offer God and He is unable to get our inheritance to us because there is no way for the two worlds to meet and come together.

2nd Corinthians 4:18:

*So we fix our eyes not on what is seen, but on what is unseen. For what is seen is temporary, but what is unseen is eternal.*

Which brings us to the next step. The second thing you need to turn this entire curse around and be eternally hooked to the blessing is to get in blood covenant with the Father. Covenant is step two. It is how we can live in a horizontal world vertically! And it was done at the cross.

Gal 3:7 NIV

*Understand, then, that those who have faith are children of Abraham.*

Aren't we in blood covenant with God when we are born? Aren't we made by Him and considered his children? Not necessarily.

When Adam and Eve fell in the garden, we were all cursed. Way back in the beginning of the bible in Genesis chapter 3.

Genesis 3:16-19 (NIV)

*To the woman he said,*

*"I will greatly increase your pains in childbearing; with pain you will give birth to children.*

*Your desire will be for your husband, and he will rule over you."*

*To Adam he said, "Because you listened to your wife and ate from the tree about which I commanded you, 'you must not eat of it,'*

*Cursed is the ground because of you; through painful toil you will eat of it all the days of your life. It will produce thorns and thistles for you, and you will eat the plants of the field. By the sweat of your brow you will eat your food until you return to the ground, since from it you were taken; for dust you are and to dust you will return."*

Because Adam and Eve ate the forbidden fruit, everyone on the planet was part of the curse, until Abraham (also named Abram) and God entered into a blood covenant.

Genesis 15:5-10 (NIV)

*He took him outside and said, "Look up at the heavens and count the stars-if indeed you can count them," Then he said to him, "so shall your offspring be." Abram believed the Lord, and he credited it to him as righteousness. He also said to him, "I am the Lord, who brought you out of Ur of the Chaldeans to give you this land to take possession of it." So the Lord said to him, "Bring me a heifer, a goat, and a ram, each three years old, along with a dove and a young pigeon." Abram brought all these to him, but them in tow and arranged the halves opposite each other.*

Genesis 15:18-20

***On that day the Lord made a covenant with Abram and said, "To your descendants I give this land, from the river of Egypt to the great river, the Euphrates-the land of the Kenites, Kenizzites, Kadmonites, hitties, Perizzites, Rephaites, Amorites, Canaanites, Girgashites, and Jebusites."***

So if you are Abrahams seed, then you are considered to be in blood covenant with the Father. Why is this significant? Blood covenants are eternal. Blood covenants cannot be broken. Although all of us have a deep awareness of God, we are human and we have faults. And if we aren't in blood covenant, an unbreakable covenant with God, then we fall short. Period. Because there is nothing permanently hooking us to His power.

Who are Abrahams seed? The Jewish. By birth they are in covenant with the Father. They don't have to do anything to be part of this promise; they only need to be born a Jew. A Jew by blood.

Genesis 12:1-3 (NASB)

***Now the LORD said to Abram, "Go forth from your country, and from your relative and from your father's house,***

*To the land which I will show you and I will make you a great nation, and I will bless you, and make your name great;*

*And so you shall be a blessing; and I will bless those who bless you,*

*and the one who curses you I will curse*

*And in you all the families of the earth will be blessed."*

What about the rest of us? AHA. I thought you'd wonder about that. This is where Jesus comes in and saves the rest of the world. It was done at the cross. And Jesus was part of the plan from the very beginning. God had already put in to motion the backup plan...it was Jesus. Because He knew we all needed a backup.

Galatians 3:14 (NIV)

*He redeemed us in order that the blessing given to Abraham might come to the Gentiles through Christ Jesus, so that by faith we might receive the promise of the Spirit.*

Galatians 3:16 (NIV)

*The promises were spoken to Abraham and to his seed. The Scripture does not say "and to seeds," meaning many people, but "and to your seed," meaning one person, who is Christ.*

What is a sacrifice? It is an offering of food or an object to God. In the old covenant between Abraham and God, a lamb was offered as the sacrifice to God. This covenant is unbreakable as long as blood is shed. So every generation of the Jewish continues in this covenant because they are related by blood. Jesus was born a Jew. He had to be because he had to be part of the old covenant by blood to make a new one. He had to be the seed of Abraham that God foretold in the first book of the Bible-in Genesis. But He also had to be God. He had to be born of God as a Jew to keep with the old covenant while offering the rest of us a way to supernaturally enter into the covenant as well. If Jesus had been beamed down from Heaven and no blood was shed in his birth, then he could not be part of the covenant of Abraham. God could have done that. He certainly has that power. The reason why He didn't is because Jesus was sent to become the blood sacrifice for a new covenant between us and God. Jesus used his body to be broken, to be the sacrificial lamb for a covenant between us and God. Jesus came to bring the rest of us into the family of Abraham. By blood. And He did this by becoming half God and half man. It was the only way.

Hebrews 9:12-14 (NIV): *He did not enter by means of the blood of goats and calves; but he entered the Most Holy Place once for all by his own blood, having obtained eternal redemption. The blood of goats and bulls and the ashes of a heifer sprinkled on those who are ceremonially unclean sanctify them so that they are outwardly clean. How much more, then, will the blood of Christ, who through the eternal Spirit offered himself unblemished to God, cleanse our consciences from acts that lead to death, so that we may serve the living God!*

Galatians 3:29 (NIV): *If you belong to Christ, then you are Abraham's seed, and heirs according to the promise.*

And it goes back to what I had written in the previous chapter, you can receive Jesus and still keep whatever religion you have. Jesus is a blood sacrifice, was sent by God so that we can all be reconciled to Him and become qualified for His promises, and is the only thing we need to have for eternal life. God never intended any of us to let our religions stop us from receiving the ultimate sacrifice of Jesus. Jesus is for us all.

Romans 5:9-11 (NIV)

*Since we have now been justified by his blood, how much more shall we be saved from God's wrath through him! For if, when we were God's enemies, we were reconciled to him through the death of his Son, how much more, having been reconciled, shall we be saved through his life! Not only is this so, but we also rejoice in God through our Lord Jesus Christ, through whom we have now received reconciliation.*

But it doesn't end there. Once you receive salvation through Jesus, you are able to walk out God's will for your life as you now enter into a personal relationship with the Father. Jesus is kind of like a mediator to God. Jesus is a "power of attorney". God, being the ultimate Judge, allows Jesus to sit at His right hand and it is Jesus who intervenes for all of us who receive Him.

Romans 8:33-34 (NIV)

*Who will bring any charge against those whom God has chosen? It is God who justifies. Who is he that condemns? Christ Jesus, who died—more than that, who was raised to life—is at the right hand of God and is also interceding for us.*

The Jewish don't need to go through Jesus to qualify for God's promises because they are part of the old covenant. They are naturally born into covenant with God. There are some Jewish believers I know that have received Jesus. Jesus came for everyone and the Jewish certainly have the same rights as any of us to receive him. However it is the rest of us, the non-Jewish that need to go through Jesus to be saved and have the life we were designed to live. Gentiles were not naturally born into blood covenant with God...we are not part of the Abraham bloodline. God couldn't get us in because we weren't qualified. The only way to get us in was to offer us a way to join the bloodline. If He had made a new covenant separate from the one of Abraham then it would have cancelled out the old

61

covenant and voided out the promise God gave him. God doesn't do that. What God says lasts forever. He could not bring us into the Kingdom with Him any other way. Or else it would have broken the first promise to Abraham. And it would have broken God's own laws for himself. He can't break His laws. So there was simply no other way.

Who are the Gentiles? Probably most of you reading this book. You can be Catholic, Muslim, Methodist, Buddhist, Christian, Jehovah's Witness, a Satanist...pretty much any other religion and be considered a Gentile. There are many more of us Gentiles than there are Jewish. We need to go through the blood of Jesus to receive the promises that are in the bible for us to have. And we do this by receiving salvation. Salvation brings all religions together.

Galatians 3:17-18 (NIV)

*The law, introduced 430 years later, does not set aside the covenant previously established by God and thus do away with the promise. For if the inheritance depends on the law, then it no longer depends on a promise; but God in his grace gave it to Abraham through a promise.*

Galatians 3:24-29 (NIV)

*You are all sons of God through faith in Christ Jesus, for all of you who were baptized into Christ have clothed yourselves with Christ. There is neither Jew nor Greek, slave nor free, male nor female, for you are all one in Christ Jesus. If you belong to Christ, then you are Abraham's seed, and heirs according to the promise.*

There is no religion that can keep you from receiving Jesus. It is between you and God. It is private and can be done anywhere at any time. Jesus will take you as you are, even if you are in the biggest and deepest pit of your life. You don't need to have your horizontal life perfect before you begin to live vertically. You simply need to have the two intersect so they can become one. And that is done through the sacrifice of Jesus. That is done through receiving Him. You have been given a great mediator to God through Jesus and are able to get all you desire through Him. It is just that simple. Jesus didn't die so you could make a new religion…he died to reconcile ALL people in ALL religions. He died so that we could live. All of us. He died so that we could help each other. And through helping each other, we activate the love of God and He is able to bring us into the blessed life. God is not limited by religion. He is bigger than all religions. And quite simply, he gave you and I Jesus so we could know Him, regardless of where we come from, what color we are, or what religion we follow.

Let me explain it another way. Without Jesus, we are all held prisoners to sin-all of us. There are two different jail cells that you can choose to live in. The jail cell of "sin" is the cell that all of us are part of from the moment we were born. Although we can go out and do excellent things, we are still contained by the cell of "sin". So even our best efforts are done futily because we remain imprisoned in sin. Once you receive salvation by accepting Jesus Christ as Lord, you step into a new jail cell. You get transferred to another entire prison. Only this prison is quite different from the prison of "sin". This jail cell is the cell of "righteousness" and there is nothing you need to do in this cell. The "righteousness" you are living is not your own doing. You are imprisoned in a cell because of the righteousness of Jesus. So even when you mess up and say a wrong thing, or have a bad attitude, you remain a prisoner of righteousness. And just like your good deeds did not carry weight in your cell of "sin", your mistakes and failures do not matter when you are in the cell of "righteousness". There is simply nothing you can do to earn your way out of "sin" or earn your way out of "righteousness". Jesus came to break us all out of our jail cell. He is the only one who has the power to get us out of "sin" and into "righteousness". There is only the choice of which prison you prefer to live in. And there is only one transfer allowed!

You can have Jesus and still follow the five pillars of the Islam faith (they aren't bad rules, you know). You can have Jesus and still celebrate the Catholic traditions and customs you grew up with. You can have Jesus and still meditate. You can have Jesus and remain in the church you attend. If God doesn't approve of something your religion is practicing, He will work on it with you once you receive Jesus. No one has the right to tell you that what you practice in your religion is wrong. None of us know for sure if we are even right. The only thing the Bible says about religion is that Jesus came for all of us. It doesn't say "excluding the following religions…"

*Isaiah 49:6I*

*will also make you a light for the Gentiles,*
*that my salvation may reach to the*

*ENDS OF THE EARTH."*

*Luke 3:5-7*

*Every valley shall be filled in,*
*every mountain and hill made low.*
*The crooked roads shall become straight,*
*the rough ways smooth.*
*⁶ And ALL PEOPLE will see God's salvation."'[a]*

*Acts 13:47*

*For this is what the Lord has commanded us:*

*"'I have made you a light for the Gentiles,*
*that you may bring salvation to the*

*ENDS OF THE EARTH.¹"*

Jesus died so that we can live glorious, prosperous, powerful, successful lives. He died so that all of us could get into a supernatural and powerful relationship with God. He died to break down the walls of containment that are set up by religions. He died so that we could overcome any obstacle put in our path by receiving the "extension cord" to God's power-Jesus and so we could break free of religion.

Religion was never intended to separate us from one another. When we are separated, then we are cut off from the power of God. Because God dwells inside of each one of us. When we share and we love one another then we are being like God to each other. Religion was set up to bring laws and standards in to help us follow God but has instead been our absolute downfall. Religion was established by man in an attempt to keep us from doing the wrong things and from going down the wrong path. But God never intended for us to go to a church or religious function to get to Him. He never wanted us to start a business out of religion. He never planned for us to bring our money to a building and drop our tithe in a bucket to fund a business or be asked for money every time we sit in front of a preacher to hear God's word. His plan was never about religion. His plan for our money was about helping others. His plan for us was about giving us power. And the only way you can get this power is by going through Him to receive it.

Luke 10:19 (NIV)

*I have given you authority to trample on snakes and scorpions and to overcome all the power of the enemy; nothing will harm you.*

If you don't have that power-that authority, then it is time to pray and ask God to save you. And believe in your heart that Jesus died on the cross so you could live. Believe that Jesus died so you can be forgiven of your sins…all of them. It is not and never was about religion. It was about blood covenant right from the beginning.

Which now brings us to the third step. How do we talk to God to make our requests? And how do we hear back from Him? How do we begin to live vertically?

The third step is communication: communication with God. This is done through spending time in prayer and spending time reading the bible.

Matthew 21:22 (NIV)

*If you believe, you will receive whatever you ask for in prayer."*

2$^{nd}$ Timothy 3:16 (NIV)

*All Scripture is God-breathed and is useful for teaching, rebuking, correcting and training in righteousness,*

Some people do this by spending time in church. Others enjoy alone time with God right in the comfort of their home. And even others spend time in prayer and read their bibles in the front seat of their car. It doesn't matter how you come to God. As long as you visit with Him. He created all types of avenues to get His word to us. Today, technology has taken us further into God's word and deeper into the Holy Scriptures than ever before. Leaving us with the only excuse that is true for not spending time with God-you simply don't want to.

If I died tomorrow and 1 million people knew me, would I be able to say that I knew all 1 million of them? No. The only people I would know would be the ones I regularly had some kind of communication with. It is the same way with God. He knows all mankind in some capacity, but it is the ones He regularly communicates with that He really knows…and this is done through prayer and through reading the Bible.

The closer you get in a relationship with someone, the better you get to know that person. It is the same thing with God. If you desire to know Him deeper, then you must spend time with Him to gain a closer relationship. Have you ever met someone who becomes so close to you that you can finish his/her sentences? How do you get that close? I had a few best friends in high school I was that close with. We were like that because we spent many hours together daily. It didn't start out that way, but it ended up there as we accumulated many hours of together time. Would you like to have that same intimacy with the creator of Heaven and Earth? Spend time with Him in his word and in prayer, and soon you will be finishing His sentences too!

## Matthew 25: 31-46 (NIV)

*"When the Son of Man comes in his glory, and all the angels with him, he will sit on his glorious throne. All the nations will be gathered before him, and he will separate the people one from another as a shepherd separates the sheep from the goats. He will put the sheep on his right and the goats on his left.*

*"Then the King will say to those on his right, 'Come, you who are blessed by my Father; take your inheritance, the kingdom prepared for you since the creation of the world. For I was hungry and you gave me something to eat, I was thirsty and you gave me something to drink, I was a stranger and you invited me in, I needed clothes and you clothed me, I was sick and you looked after me, I was in prison and you came to visit me.'*

*"Then the righteous will answer him, 'Lord, when did we see you hungry and feed you, or thirsty and give you something to drink?* [38] *When did we see you a stranger and invite you in, or needing clothes and clothe you?* [39] *When did we see you sick or in prison and go to visit you?'*

*"The King will reply, 'Truly I tell you, whatever you did for one of the least of these brothers and sisters of mine, you did for me.'*

*"Then he will say to those on his left, 'Depart from me, you who are cursed, into the eternal fire prepared for the devil and his angels. For I was hungry and you gave me nothing to eat, I was thirsty and you gave me nothing to drink, I was a stranger and you did not invite me in, I needed clothes and you did not clothe me, I was sick and in prison and you did not look after me.'*

*"They also will answer, 'Lord, when did we see you hungry or thirsty or a stranger or needing clothes or sick or in prison, and did not help you?'*

*"He will reply, 'Truly I tell you, whatever you did not do for one of the least of these, you did not do for me.'*

*"Then they will go away to eternal punishment, but the righteous to eternal life."*

Be careful to end up on the "right" side…

# A FOND FAREWELL

Well, that does it. I am finished with another book. I shall bid you farewell until I write another. But this one in particular has quite a special place in my heart. I want to thank you for reading it and allowing me to speak into your life. It is always an honor.

I began this book with taxation and the church heavy on my mind. As I wrote the pages however, God turned me once again to write for Him and speak of Jesus and his sacrifice. God wants all His children to come back to Him; to get in blood covenant with Him through Jesus. And if you didn't know the true living God before you read this book, I hope that you will spend time getting to know Him now. He misses you. And He wants you to come back home so you can rest.

Today I am in my living room typing away on my "lucky laptop". But as I sit here I am joyfully reminded of the reason I do what I do. 6 young boys are gathered on my couch watching a movie together. They are part of my ministry, called the Littlest Mission. The children in The Littlest Mission range in age from 4 to 16. They will be in South Africa this summer to dig wells for children that have never had any running water. And the following summer they will be heading to Pakistan to help bring peace between Muslim and American children by breaking down religious barriers and spreading God's love. They are just beginning their journey with God. These kids are going to change the world some day. All the kids. They will do things that have never been done before. These children will become doctors, lawyers, teachers, and politicians. They will invent new gadgets, vote on new laws, and stand tall for what they believe is right in their heart. These kids we are raising today are going to change the world. And it is crucial that we make the right changes today to affect their lives tomorrow.

I hope that the message in this book goes deep into your heart. I hope that you have been challenged to look at church and God a little differently, and that you've learned to think outside the box. I pray that I have made God a little more tangible to you, and that you continue to grow closer to Him the rest of the days of your life.

For it is God who directed the words in this book, and it is because of Him alone that I am able to write. Thank you from the bottom of my heart for helping me to change the world for these kids, and affect the future of this great country. I am going to finish with a few scriptures and leave you with some of God's word.

Romans 12:1-3 (NIV)

*Therefore, I urge you, brothers, in view of God's mercy, to offer your bodies as living sacrifices, holy and pleasing to God—this is your spiritual act of worship. Do not conform any longer to the pattern of this world, but be transformed by the renewing of your mind. Then you will be able to test and approve what God's will is—his good, pleasing and perfect will.*

Joshua 24:14-16 (NIV)

*"Now fear the LORD and serve him with all faithfulness. Throw away the gods your forefathers worshiped beyond the River and in Egypt, and serve the LORD. But if serving the LORD seems undesirable to you, then choose for yourselves this day whom you will serve, whether the gods your forefathers served beyond the River, or the gods of the Amorites, in whose land you are living. But as for me and my household, we will serve the LORD."*

And my favorite verse in the Bible—

Colossians 1:17 (NIV)

*He is before all things, and in him all things hold together.*

**Thank you so much and God Bless!**

# REFERENCES:

Bruce, F.F. et al. *The Origin of the Bible,* United States, Tyndale House 1992. Print.

Cline Austin. *Tax Exemptions Available to Churches, Tax Exemptions and Religion.* About.com Guide. Retrieved from atheism.about.com. web.

http://atheism.about.com/od/churchestaxexemptions/a/churchexempti on.htm Used with written permission from Austin Cline-Guide to Agnosticism / Atheism. http://atheism.about.com

Internal Revenue Service. Retrieved from irs.gov. www.irs.gov/pub/irs-utl/branch_ministries.pdf

Jacobsen Jeff.*Scientology's Tax Exemption Should be Rescinded.* July 19, 2001. Retrieved from lisamcpherson.org Web.

http://www.lisamcpherson.org/irs/jeff-irs.htm

Murray Jean. *US Business Law/Tax Guide.* Retrieved from biztxlaw.about.com.webhttp://biztaxlaw.about.com/b/2009/04/03/ how-much-tax-do-businesses-pay.htm

Scott Jeffrey Warren. *Taxing Church Property: An Imminent Possibility?* Retrieved from religion-online.com. Web. http://www.religion-online.org/showarticle.asp?title=1030

wikipedia.com, the free encyclopedia. 501(c). Retrieved from wikipedia.com http://en.wikipedia.org/wiki/501(c)#501.28c.29.283.29

wikipedia.com, the free encyclopedia. *Pluralism.* Retrieved from wikipedia.com http://en.wikipedia.org/wiki/Pluralism

wikipedia.com, the free encyclopedia. *First Amendment to the United States Constitution.* Retrieved from wikipedia.com http://en.wikipedia.org/wiki/First_Amendment_to_the_United States_Constitution

Wilson, R. *Artaxerxes.* Retrieved from net.bible.org. http://net.bible.org/dictionary.php?word=Artaxerxes. Web

"The Federalist Papers". Retrieved from

foundingfathers.info.

http://www.foundingfathers.info/federalistpapers/

# PERMISSIONS

Scripture quotations marked (NIV) are taken from the
Holy Bible, New International Version®, NIV®.
Copyright © 1973, 1978, 1984 by Biblica, Inc.™
Used by permission of Zondervan. All rights reserved
worldwide.

www.zondervan.com

Scripture quotations marked (KJV) are taken from the
Holy Bible King    James Version.

Scripture quotations marked (TLB) are taken from The
Living Bible    copyright 1971 owned by assignment
by NNT Charitable Trust.  All rights    reserved.

All scripture was originally written by God.  So if I missed
any it doesn't matter.  Because ultimately none of these
publishers own any of it.  No copyrights, no rights
reserved.  BLAH BLAH BLAH (yes, I had to get in
the last word).